THE FALL OF QUEBEC

QUEBEC

AND THE FRENCH AND INDIAN WAR

Turning Points
IN AMERICAN HISTORY

THE FALL OF QUEBEC

AND THE FRENCH AND INDIAN WAR

George Ochoa

Silver Burdett Press, Inc.
Englewood Cliffs, New Jersey

Acknowledgments

The author thanks Melinda Corey for her help in reviewing and editing this volume. The editor thanks the following individuals and institutions for their invaluable help in text and picture research: Mr. Paul Castle, the New Brunswick Museum; C.E.W. Graham, McCord Museum, McGill University; and Ms. Edna Rodriguez, the Public Archives of Canada.

Consultants

We thank the following people for reviewing the manuscript and offering their helpful suggestions:

Karen E. Markoe
Professor of History
Maritime College of
the State University of New York

Robert M. Goldberg
Department Chairman, Social Studies
Team Leader of Interdisciplinary
Group of Academic Teachers
Oceanside Middle School
Oceanside, New York

Cover: British troops storm Quebec on September 13, 1759. National Archives of Canada/c-10708, hand-colored by Simon Hu.

Title Page: The Battle of the Plains of Abraham, 1759, painted by George Campion. National Archives of Canada/c-4501.

Contents Page: A Wampum belt commemorating a 1701 treaty between the French and the Iroquois. McCord Museum of Canadian History, Montreal.

Back Cover: This painting depicts British General Edward Braddock's 1755 defeat near the forks of the Ohio River. Courtesy of the State Historical Society of Wisconsin.

Library of Congress Cataloging-in-Publication Data

Ochoa, George.
 The fall of Quebec and the French and Indian War/George Ochoa.
  p. cm. —(Turning points in American History.)
 Includes bibliographical references.
 Summary: Describes the people, places, and events surrounding the French and Indian War.
 1. Quebec Campaign, 1759—Juvenile literature. [1. United States—History—French and Indian War, 1755-1763.] I. Title. II. Series: Turning points in American history.
E199.027 1990
973.2'6—dc20   90-8420
                        CIP
                        AC

Editorial Coordination by Richard G. Gallin

 Created by Media Projects Incorporated

C. Carter Smith, *Executive Editor*
Toni Rachiele, *Managing Editor*
Charles A. Wills, *Project Editor*
Bernard Schleifer, *Design Consultant*
Arlene Goldberg, *Cartographer*

ISBN 0-382-09954-0 [lib. bdg.]
10 9 8 7 6 5 4 3 2 1

ISBN 0-382-09950-8 [pbk.]
10 9 8 7 6 5 4 3 2 1

CONTENTS

INTRODUCTION

THE CLIFFS

Just before dawn on a calm night in September 1759, a boat filled with British soldiers touched the shore of the St. Lawrence River about two miles west of Quebec. The soldiers dashed silently out of the boat while other boats landed behind them. Above them stretched a wall of cliffs 175 feet high. These heights had kept the French Canadian city of Quebec safe from capture for 130 years.

Not far from where the boats landed was a narrow path. A hundred Quebec militiamen (citizen soldiers) guarded the path, and an *abatis*—a barrier made from felled trees with sharpened branches—blocked the way. The only other way to reach the top was by climbing the rocky face of the cliff. Colonel William Howe, the thirty-year-old commander of the British light infantry, decided to do just that.

Victorious British troops line up in front of Quebec's cathedral.

Howe led his men up the steep slope. Their only handholds were bushes and small trees. Below them in the darkness, the river thundered; above them the stars shone. They reached the top and crept toward the French camp. A sentry challenged them; they stopped. A member of the British forces, a Scotsman who spoke French, made up a story. He said he had come to relieve the sentry and his fellow troops along the cliff. The sentry seemed to believe him, but suddenly the air was filled with musket shots. Someone had gotten nervous and fired.

The battle didn't last long. Many of the militiamen had been asleep, and were too startled to put up a good fight. Some of the French soldiers were taken prisoner; the rest escaped. The British now controlled the path up the cliff.

The *abatis* blocking the path was cleared away. British troops swarmed up the path. On the river below, the oars and rowlocks of thirty boats

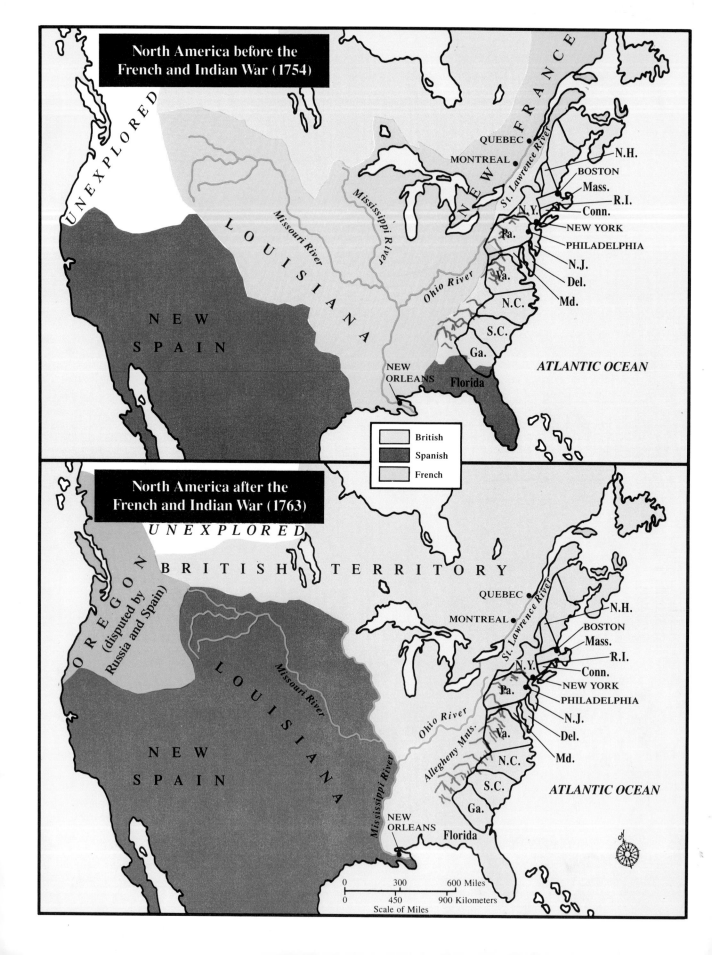

North America before the French and Indian War (1754)

UNEXPLORED

NEW SPAIN

LOUISIANA

Missouri River

Mississippi River

Ohio River

NEW FRANCE

St. Lawrence River

QUEBEC

MONTREAL

N.H.

BOSTON

Mass.

R.I.

Conn.

N.Y.

NEW YORK

PHILADELPHIA

N.J.

Del.

Md.

Pa.

Va.

N.C.

S.C.

Ga.

Florida

NEW ORLEANS

ATLANTIC OCEAN

British

Spanish

French

North America after the French and Indian War (1763)

UNEXPLORED

BRITISH TERRITORY

OREGON (disputed by Russia and Spain)

NEW SPAIN

LOUISIANA

Missouri River

Mississippi River

Ohio River

Allegheny Mnts.

St. Lawrence River

QUEBEC

MONTREAL

N.H.

BOSTON

Mass.

R.I.

Conn.

N.Y.

NEW YORK

PHILADELPHIA

N.J.

Del.

Md.

Pa.

Va.

N.C.

S.C.

Ga.

Florida

NEW ORLEANS

ATLANTIC OCEAN

0   300   600 Miles
0   450   900 Kilometers
Scale of Miles

Wolfe's volunteers climb up the slope.

creaked as the men came ashore. Floating down the river came larger ships—armed sloops, frigates, transports crammed with soldiers. Field cannon were unloaded and pulled up the path. As the French farther along the cliff realized what was happening, they fired a battery (a group of cannon) at the ships. British soldiers crept up and captured the battery. The landing continued.

The sun rose as the British assembled on the cliff. They formed in red-coated regiments, their backs to the river, the city of Quebec to their right.

Their commander, Major-General James Wolfe, reviewed their ranks. Wolfe was thirty-two years old, tall and lanky, with a shock of bright red hair. He was weak with sickness, but he had just carried out one of the most brilliant military operations ever accomplished. In about two hours, in darkness, he had led an army of 4,500 troops over an obstacle considered impassable. Yet the day had only just begun. The city of Quebec was still unconquered.

The battle that followed was the turning point of Great Britain's war with

See here O fair Britania at thy Feet:
The Gallic Genius does her Keys submit.
The Standards too of her proud boasting band:
She supliant brings with her submissive hands:
When the brave Wolfe heroic, led the Way.
To Victory, and dying, won the Day;
Which brought them under George's milder sway.

Quebec no more is hers, Auspicious Heav'n!
Has that to Britains braver Genius given;
No more Acadian Swains, beneath the pow'r
Of Tyrants groan, but bless the happy Hour.

Cobin delin.

How just the fa
The Conqueror
Not the Sea
Nor all her C

Publish'd according to Act of Parliament.

France in North America. That war was one part of a much larger conflict, which raged in many parts of the world from 1756 to 1763. Great Britain and Prussia fought on one side; France, Austria, Russia, Sweden, and several German states on the other. The conflict is known by some as the Seven Years' War because the war in Europe lasted from 1756 to 1763. Others call it the Great War

GEORGIUS · SECUNDUS · PRIN · OPT · PATER PATRIÆ

Serus in Cœlum redeas diuque
Lætus interfis Populo Britaniæ.

Hulet sculp.

w much to him is owing | Of her fire belching Cannon could affright
sbourg. Boscawen; | The Sailors souls, resolv'd to die, or right
ng on her rocky Shore. | Britanias Wrongs; Not so thy Gallic Host
nor th' impetuous roar. | For thee can fight, Louis, with all thy boast
They now can chatter, dance, and run away.
But leave to Us the Honour of the Day.
So have I seen a flock of silly Geese.
Dare at Jove's Bird, to clap their Wings & hiss,
But if he stoop'd the Insult to resent!
On nought but fright & flight, the cackling Host were bent.

In this engraving, defeated France kneels to victorious Britain after the French and Indian War.

British colonies that later became the United States. Until the French and Indian War, France and England were about equally powerful in North America. Each controlled vast regions. Each had dealings with the Native Americans who already occupied the land—sometimes peaceful dealings, sometimes violent. Life in each country's colonies was very different, but each wanted to expand its holdings. In the end, only one could.

France was defeated in the French and Indian War. Britain took over most of France's American empire, including the province known as Canada. But Britain's victory was short-lived. That was because the war also marked a turning point in the American colonies' relationship with Britain. Thirteen years later, as a result of grievances made worse by the French and Indian War, Britain's original colonies declared themselves "free and independent states." In the revolution that followed, Britain kept Canada but lost its original colonies. These became the United States.

The French and Indian War reached its turning point when General Wolfe's army assembled on the cliffs west of Quebec. The seeds of the great war were sown nearly 200 years earlier, when the first Europeans from rival countries set foot on North American soil.

for Empire. In North America, where the war began, it is most often called the French and Indian War.

Whatever one calls it, the war had important consequences for the thirteen

1

RIVALS IN THE NEW WORLD

In the spring of 1534, two ships from France sailed into the Gulf of St. Lawrence, at the eastern tip of what is now Canada. Commanded by Jacques Cartier, the ships had been sent by the French king to look for a short route to the riches of China. They never found that route, but they opened the way to what would one day be an empire.

Cartier, a master sailor, was not the first European to explore the region. As early as the tenth century, the Vikings of northern Europe tried to settle in Newfoundland at the entrance to the gulf. Since then, Giovanni Caboto, also known as John Cabot, had mapped parts of the area for England. French fishermen sailed every summer to fish in the rich waters. But as yet, no European had traveled very far into Canada.

Jacques Cartier sites the land that became New France.

Near the place where the mighty St. Lawrence River spills into the gulf, Cartier met about forty canoes filled with Huron tribesmen. To the French captain, the Hurons were savage-looking—wearing only furs and loincloths, their heads shaved except for a knot of hair at the top. To the Hurons, the Europeans must have looked equally strange. But the Hurons were eager to trade for European goods.

Cartier's sailors raised a cross 30 feet tall on the shore. On it was written "Long Live the King of France." Cartier sailed back to France, after completing the first documented circuit of the Gulf of St. Lawrence. With him went two Hurons, teenage sons of the chief. These young men told stories of a fabulous Kingdom of Saguenay, where gold and precious stones abounded. Saguenay was no more real than the shortcut to China—the so-called Northwest Passage—that had brought Cartier out the

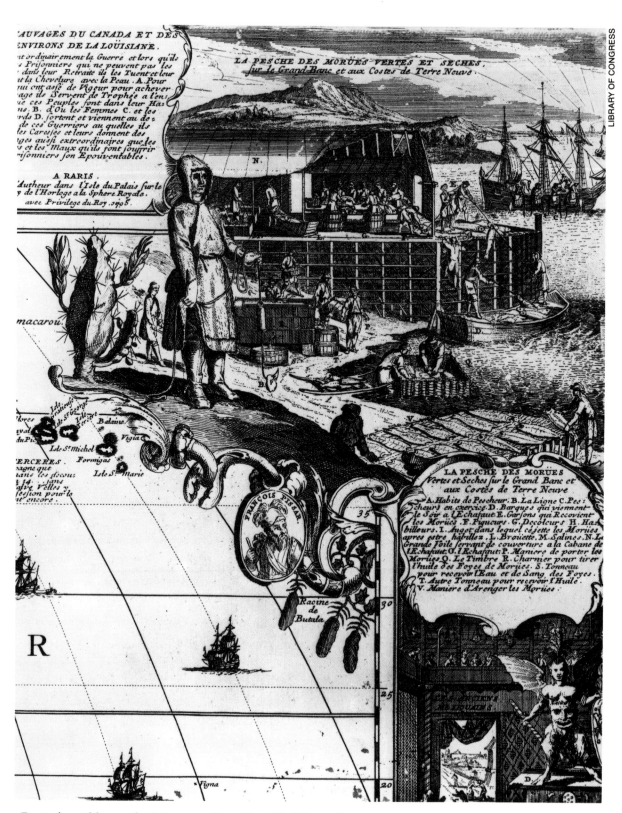

Part of an old map depicts scenes from the rich fishery of the Grand Banks.

first time. But the hope of finding it encouraged him to return on a second voyage.

The region that Cartier now explored, with the two young Hurons as guides, was one of great natural beauty. At the mouth of the St. Lawrence River, the banks were rocky and wooded. In his account of the voyage, Cartier described beluga, small white whales "with head like a greyhound," and walruses, "fish with the shape of horses." Cartier traveled against the current up the St. Lawrence River until he reached the Huron camp, where the chief was reunited with his sons. The Hurons then brought the French for the first time to the rock of Quebec.

It was not called Quebec then. It was a promontory, a high point of rock between the small St. Charles River and the great St. Lawrence. At the base of the cliffs was the Huron village of Stadacona. Cartier left the place and kept searching for the Kingdom of Saguenay. He never found it, but he explored the St. Lawrence River as far as the rapids near present-day Montreal.

In 1541, Cartier returned one last time, this time with several shiploads of colonists. They spent the winter at a settlement near Quebec but found life there brutally hard. For five months, snow surrounded their camp and ice blocked the St. Lawrence. Many colonists died of illness. The king of France decided he had sponsored enough voyages to Canada.

The story of French settlement in the New World might have ended there except for an unexpected source of wealth—the beaver. This new resource was first tapped by the French seamen who fished every summer off the "Grand Banks" of Newfoundland. Native Americans offered these fishermen beaver furs in exchange for metal goods such as knives, axes, and kettles. It turned out that the furs could be made into handsome, durable hats. By 1600, the hats had become popular across Europe. The king of France decided there was wealth to be had in North America after all. A fashion trend had changed history.

In 1603, the king of France gave a monopoly—sole rights to gather fur in Canada—to Pierre du Gua, Sieur de Monts, on the condition that de Monts found a colony in Canada. One colony was founded at Port Royal on a spur of land called Acadia, now Nova Scotia. In 1608, de Monts's lieutenant, a soldier and seaman named Samuel de Champlain, led twenty-four colonists to the very cliffs that Jacques Cartier had visited 75 years earlier. At the base of those cliffs Champlain founded the colony of Quebec on July 3, 1608. This colony of Quebec succeeded where Cartier's had failed.

At about the same time, France's European rivals were also founding settlements in North America. Spain, which had conquered almost all of South America and Central America, founded St. Augustine in Florida in 1565 and Santa Fe in New Mexico in 1609. In 1607, the English founded Jamestown, in Virginia. In the 1620s, the Dutch

This 1613 woodcut depicts Samuel Champlain's "habitation" at Quebec.

settled at Fort Orange and New Amsterdam in what is now New York. Also in the 1620s, English Separatists and Puritans founded Plymouth and Massachusetts Bay in what became New England.

Like most of these colonies, Quebec suffered many hardships in its first years. Food was scarce and winters were harsh; in the first year, sixteen of twenty-four colonists died. The colony was tiny, with only three connected buildings surrounded by a wooden wall, or stockade. But Champlain refused to let New France die. He sought out the help of the Native Americans with whom the French traded—the Hurons and the Algonkian tribes. In return, these tribes asked Champlain to help them in their wars.

Both the Hurons and the Algonkian had been at war for years with the Iroquois League. The league was an alliance of five Native American nations (the Cayuga, the Mohawk, the Oneida, the Onondaga, and the Seneca). The Iroquois lived in what is now central New York State; their neighbors, the Hurons, lived in what is now the Canadian province of Ontario. The Algonkian tribes—which included the Algonkin, the Montagnais, the Ottawa, and the Abnaki—ranged across what is now the American Midwest and as far east as Maine. The Huron-Algonkian and the Iroquois fought for many reasons—prestige, power, revenge, land. With the arrival of the French came a new reason: control of the fur trade with Europe.

In July 1609, Champlain and two other Frenchmen accompanied a band of sixty Algonkian warriors to what is now called Lake Champlain, on the border between New York and Vermont. There, with the help of firearms—a new and frightening sight to the Iroquois—the Algonkian defeated an Iroquois force nearly three times larger. The alliance between the French and the Huron-Algonkian was sealed. The French and the Iroquois now become lasting enemies.

The French and their Native American allies both benefited from their alliance. From the Native Americans, the French learned to grow crops such as corn, pumpkin, and squash. Native Americans offered tools perfectly suited to life in the woods—birchbark canoes, snowshoes, toboggans or sleds. Native

This painting, Dance for the Recovery of the Sick *by George Heriot, shows a traditional Native American ceremony.*

Americans served as guides and taught French explorers how to survive in the forest. Native Americans, for their part, received European goods—steel knives and kettles, woolen blankets, guns. A few powerful tribes, such as the Hurons, earned an especially good living by acting as agents of trade between the French and other tribes.

The French found that Native American combat was different from European war. Native American combat involved small numbers of warriors and took relatively few lives. But war among North American tribes had several hideous aspects. The tribes tortured prisoners of war for days, then killed them. Captured warriors showed their courage by not flinching as they were mutilated or burned. Some tribes—particularly those in the Midwest, such as the Potowatomi and the Ottawa—ate their prisoners in cannibal feasts. Many tribes scalped their enemies—a practice that might have originated in North America or been introduced by the Europeans. Most Europeans viewed the torture and scalping of prisoners with disgust but learned to use these practices as tools of terror against their own enemies.

As early as 1613, the French became involved in European as well as Native American rivalries in the New World. In that year, Captain Samuel Argall of the English colony of Virginia wiped out the French settlements in Acadia and what is now Maine. In the years that followed, England and France often

Champlain and the Hurons battle the Iroquois.

fought over the fur trade and the "Great Fishery" of the Gulf of St. Lawrence. In 1629, the English captured Quebec and forced Champlain to evacuate. Not until 1633, after peace was signed, did Champlain return—just two years before he died in the colony he had founded. The English remained nearby in New England and on the shores of Hudson Bay, a great inland sea northwest of Quebec.

The Dutch in the Hudson River Valley (in present-day New York) also threatened France's control of the fur trade. In 1615, the rivalry between the French and the Dutch merged with the war between the Algonkian and the Iroquois. Near what is now Syracuse, New York, Champlain was wounded in battle with Iroquois fighting as allies of the Dutch. Raiding parties of the Iroquois soon attacked French settlements along the St. Lawrence. In the 1640s, the Iroquois all but wiped out the Huron tribe—France's first ally in the New World. But after the English conquered the Dutch colonies in 1664, the Dutch were no longer allies of the Iroquois. The English were.

The European contest in the northern parts of North America had narrowed down to France and England. With their Native American allies, these two powers would struggle for control of the continent for nearly a hundred years. In that struggle, each side had different strengths and weaknesses.

The differences between the two empires were rooted in their economies—their ways of producing goods that could be traded and used. New France counted on the fur trade, while the English colonists developed many other resources. The English colonists sold crops such as tobacco, sugar, cotton, and indigo overseas. They also sold forest products such as lumber, tar, and pitch. To grow food and trade crops, the English colonies planted farms throughout the lowlands of the east coast. As a result, the English colonies could support a growing population. In 1672, the European population of the English colonies was more than 85,000. That of New France was only about 6,700.

New France grew slowly for several reasons. It had little land suitable for farming. Much of the land that was suitable was covered by forests—and the French were unwilling to cut these down. The forests were the source of beaver fur and the home of New France's Native American allies. Yet another reason for New France's slow growth was a shortage of men in France who could be sent to Canada. Throughout most of the 1600s, France was at war with its neighbors and needed troops at home.

England, however, had a surplus population—poor people who needed a place to go. In the 1500s and 1600s, many farm workers in England were driven off the land. Farmland was turned into sheep pasture to raise wool,

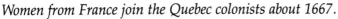
Women from France join the Quebec colonists about 1667.

A modern-day reconstruction of a seventeenth-century Roman Catholic mission in New France.

in what became known as the Enclosure Movement. As the wool industry grew, so did the numbers of the poor. Many of these came to America as indentured servants—servants who agreed to work a certain number of years in return for passage to America.

New France also stayed thinly populated because it required its colonists to be French and Catholic. French Protestants who wanted to escape persecution at home were kept out. The British colonies, on the other hand, were made up of people of many religious beliefs and nationalities. In fact, by 1763, slightly less than half of the population was English. The rest were Dutch, Swedish, Scots, Irish, German, to name a few. One-fifth were African, brought over forcibly to work as slaves.

New France made up for its small population by its good relations with Native Americans. The French followed the tradition of Champlain in treating allied tribes with fairness and respect. They tried not to disturb Native American hunting grounds. The French were generous with trade goods and sensitive to Native American concerns. In contrast, the British regarded American Indians as subhuman "savages." As they expanded, the English colonies pushed American Indians off their land, resulting in hostility and bloodshed.

The British had one strong ally among the Native Americans—the Iroquois League. However, New France's allies found that cooperation with the French brought troubles of its own. New France's allies were hurt by European diseases such as smallpox; by the spread of alcohol; by dependence on French goods; by wars over the fur trade. But in general, the French got along better with their Native American allies than the British did. One English observer wrote: "The French have found some secret of conciliating the affections [gaining the goodwill] of the savages, which our traders seem stranger to."

New France also had the advantage of a strong central organization. Under King Louis XIV, who put New France under direct royal control in 1663, Canada was ruled by a governor who answered only to the king. An official called the intendant took charge of domestic matters. The Superior Council—most of whose members were appointed by the king—made law and judged cases. Each of the British colonies, however, had a separate government, and each came to have some type of elected assembly. More people in the British colonies had a voice in government than in New France. But New France was more capable of unity in time of war.

Perhaps New France's greatest strength was its ability to travel deep inside the continent. Until the mid-eighteenth century, the westward spread of British settlement was limited by the Appalachian Mountains. That mountain range separates the lowlands of the east coast from the middle of the continent. But the French had a gateway to the heart of North America—the St. Lawrence River. That river led to other rivers, lakes, and streams. In a wilderness without roads, waterways served as paths of transportation and communication. The French made it their business to take control of these waterways.

North America's rivers and lakes were explored by many French pioneers. Some were *coureurs de bois*, or "runners of the woods"—Canadians who traveled by canoe, learned to live like Native Americans, and traded for fur in the wilderness. Others were Roman Catholic missionaries, seeking out Native Americans who might be converted to Christianity.

Traveling west from the St. Lawrence Valley, French explorers discovered the Great Lakes, the Wisconsin River, and the Illinois River. From Lake Superior they reached Lake Winnipeg and the Saskatchewan River, north of what is now North Dakota. Closer to home, they found the Ohio Valley on the western edge of what is now Pennsylvania. To the south, they found the Mississippi River. Traveling down that mighty river in 1682, Robert Cavalier de La Salle reached the Gulf of Mexico. There he raised the king's white banner and claimed the entire Mississippi Valley for France.

As New France reached deeper into the continent, and as the British colonies grew, the rivalry between the two empires increased. As New France expanded, it cut off the westward spread of the British colonies. In the Northeast, old tensions flared up over the fur trade. In Europe, new tensions arose between England and France. When fighting broke out along the New York–Canadian frontier in 1690, no one was surprised. French and English alike had entered a period of what would seem like endless war.

2

ENDLESS WAR

On a cold night in February 1690, about 200 armed men slipped through the gates of the walled village of Schenectady on the frontier of the British colony of New York. The war party was made up of Canadians and Caughnawaga—Iroquois tribesmen known as "mission Indians" because they had converted to Roman Catholicism. Without making a noise, the raiders surrounded the log cabins of the sleeping settlers. At a signal from their officers, they attacked.

The settlers woke to the sound of smashing doors and the war whoops of the Caughnawaga. Some villagers were shot or stabbed as they lay in their beds, others as they ran out into the snow. Sixty were killed, including a dozen children. Many others were taken prisoner while the village was burned to the ground.

The Schenectady Massacre *by Samuel H. Sexton.*

To the English colonists, the raid on Schenectady was an outrage that led to war. For the French Canadians, it was another battle in a war that the English had started. For both sides, it marked the beginning of a long and bitter struggle. For seventy years, war would rage in North America, broken now and then by uneasy peace. To the British colonists, the four wars fought from 1689 to 1763 would be known as King William's War (1689–1697), Queen Anne's War (1701–1713), King George's War (1744–1748), and the French and Indian War (1754–1763). As a group, they are called the French and Indian Wars.

For the French, the raid on Schenectady was part of a war already under way with the Iroquois. The Iroquois had been trying for years to break New France's control of the fur trade. In the summer of 1689, the small Canadian village of La Chine, near Montreal, was attacked by 1,500 Iroquois. They burned the village, killed many settlers, and tortured prisoners. The French believed

New France's Governor Frontenac orders an Indian tortured.

that the New York fur traders who supplied the Iroquois were responsible.

New France did not have enough troops to attack large towns, so the Canadians raided frontier settlements like Schenectady. In the coming months, the Canadians and their Native American allies wiped out settlements in New Hampshire and Maine. The French called it *la petite guerre*, "the little war." The English called it murder.

Back in Europe, the parent countries of the colonies were also at war. Under King Louis XIV, who had begun his long reign as a boy in 1643, France had become the most powerful nation in Europe. In a series of wars, Louis tried to take over neighboring lands. At first the Netherlands, France's neighbor to the northwest, stood almost alone against

him. But other countries came to believe that Louis was a danger to them as well.

In the late 1680s, the Netherlands, Austria, Spain, and other nations joined forces against France as a group called the Grand Alliance. They were led by the Dutch prince William of Orange. The English king, James II, was friendly toward France and would not declare war. But in December 1688, James was forced off the throne in what became known as the Glorious Revolution. In his place came his daughter Mary and her husband, William of Orange. In 1689, William brought England into the War of the Grand Alliance.

In America the conflict was called King William's War. As "children" of their parent countries, the French and British colonies were expected to take part. But they received little help in doing so: Europe needed its armies at home. For the most part, the colonies were on their own.

New York raised its own forces, as did New England (an area that included Massachusetts, Rhode Island, Connecticut, New Hampshire, and the district of Maine). New York and New England raised a small fleet commanded by Sir William Phips. Phips was a shipbuilder and trader who had made a fortune by finding treasure on a sunken ship. In May 1690, his fleet captured Port Royal in French Acadia. Phips then sailed against Quebec—the capital of New France. He was turned away by the army and artillery waiting for him on the cliffs.

A land army was supposed to help Phips by attacking Montreal. This force was supposed to travel through the Lake Champlain valley, which connected New York and Canada and served as a useful invasion route. But the British army was so disorganized it never even got out of New York.

Although the British colonies had more people, their weaknesses were clear. First, the French were better prepared for war. Second, the British colonies had little unity; each looked to its own interests and was jealous of the others. New France, however, was united under one governor. Also, the English militia had little formal training or experience in forest warfare. Canada's troops had both.

Still, Canada had little hope of conquering the English colonies. Canada

An early depiction of an Iroquois tribesman.

lacked a strong navy, and there were simply too many English colonists. The French had to be content with small raids—*la petite guerre*. The Abnaki of Maine, Native American allies of the French, killed many settlers in New England. They cut off the scalps of those they killed—the French paid them a price for each scalp. The British were less skilled at getting Native Americans to fight on their side, but they did organize some raids. The frontiers became a place of terror.

Meanwhile, New France's war with the Iroquois continued. The Iroquois were shot down while they hunted and fished. Iroquois villages and winter food supplies were destroyed. By 1696, disease, war, and hunger had cut the

CAPTURED

The French and Indian Wars produced several examples of a new kind of literature—the captivity narrative. In these firsthand accounts, colonists taken captive by Native Americans told of their experiences. Among the most famous narratives was the Reverend John Williams's *The Redeemed Captive Returning to Zion* (1707). In it, he told how he and his family were captured in the raid on Deerfield, Massachusetts, during Queen Anne's War.

The village of Deerfield was attacked on February 29, 1704. The raiders included Caughnawaga warriors—Iroquois converted to Catholicism by the French. About fifty settlers were killed, including two of Williams's eight children. More than a hundred settlers were taken prisoner. They were marched 300 miles back to Canada, suffering bitter cold and hunger. Those who lagged behind were killed by the tomahawk, or hatchet; one of these was Williams's wife. The minister's children, however, were treated gently. His seven-year-old daughter, Eunice, was carried in a warrior's arms all the way to Canada.

Once the captives reached Canada, their treatment improved. Williams lived in a wigwam at a mission settlement until the governor of Canada redeemed (freed) him and many other captives—paying ransom money to buy them. For more than two years, Williams lived in Canada. The French did nothing worse than try to coax him into becoming Catholic—something the Protestant minister refused to do. His greatest hardship, however, was his separation from his children.

In the fall of 1706, the captives who wanted to return were ransomed by Massachusetts. Williams and fifty-six others set sail from Quebec and arrived at Boston in November. By then, all but one of Williams's children had been ransomed from the Caughnawaga. His youngest daughter, Eunice, had not. The Caughnawaga refused to give her up because they had adopted her as one of their own.

At first, adoption was hard for Eunice. In her last meeting with her father, Williams described how she "bemoaned her state among them." He added, "She is there still; and has forgotten [how] to speak English." But Eunice learned to be happy with her new way of life. Native Americans treated their children with kindness and affection. Women enjoyed greater respect than they did in the colonies, suffering none of the beatings that many colonial wives endured. Over the years, thousands of colonists—some of them runaway slaves—were adopted into Native American tribes. Many chose to remain with the Native Americans all their lives.

Eunice married a Caughnawaga and raised two children. Years later, after her father died, she visited her relatives in Deerfield. They did not try to talk her into coming home. Her home was with her adopted tribe.

numbers of Iroquois in half. In 1701, the Iroquois signed a treaty promising to remain neutral in future wars. For a time, that treaty ended the Iroquois threat to the French—perhaps the only important result of King William's War in America.

In 1697, the warring nations of Europe made peace, without settling anything of importance. The peace proved to be only a truce while the nations gathered strength for another round. In 1701, that second round began. It was started when King Louis XIV of France placed one of his grandsons on the throne of Spain. Spain held valuable territories in Europe and a large empire in America. For France and Spain to be united under one king would upset the balance of power—it would make France too strong. England, the Netherlands, and other countries declared war. In Europe, it was called the War of the Spanish Succession. In America, it was called Queen Anne's War, after the woman who then ruled England.

Because the French and the Iroquois had agreed not to fight each other, the colony of New York—an ally of the Iroquois—was spared the raids that had marked the last war. New England was not so lucky. Again the villages of the frontier burned. Again farming and fishing families were killed and scalped. Again, the English hit back, wiping out the French settlement of Grand Pré in Acadia.

In the South, a new theater of battle opened. For several decades, the French, English, and Spanish had been

The Marquis de Vaudreuil, who governed New France as it expanded.

setting up colonies that were dangerously close to one another. French traders and soldiers were camped in the Mississippi Valley, named Louisiana after King Louis XIV. To the east of the French, the Spanish had small settlements in Florida. To the north of Florida, the English were in South Carolina. Troops from South Carolina slipped into Florida and destroyed two Spanish towns. Neither the French nor the Spanish were able to strike back effectively.

Meanwhile, leaders of the northern colonies appealed to Britain for help. In 1710, help came. Britain sent five warships and helped New England's navy capture Port Royal in Acadia. Port Royal had been taken by Phips's fleet in the last war, but it was returned to France when peace was made. This time, the English kept it. They renamed it Annapolis Royal—"Queen Anne's Town."

Once again, the British turned their eyes toward Quebec. In August 1711, seventy ships from England and the colonies reached the Gulf of St. Lawrence. They never got any farther. Lost in a dense fog, ten of the ships broke up on the rocks. Nearly a thousand men died. The commanders ordered the rest of the fleet home. Once again, Quebec had escaped capture.

In North America, the war was nearly over. For the colonies, it achieved little more than the last war. But in Europe it was of great importance. Stunning British victories broke the power of France to keep fighting. In 1713, the Peace of Utrecht ended the war and spelled the end of King Louis XIV's attempts to dominate Europe. When he died in 1715, he was a tired old man, and his country was nearly bankrupt.

Under the terms of the peace, France and Spain were to be ruled by separate monarchs. Spain's possessions in Europe were given to other countries. England gained valuable trading rights in Spanish America—including the *asiento*, a monopoly for selling African slaves. From the French, England gained Acadia—a territory that the English called Nova Scotia, or New Scotland. Still, central Canada remained in French hands. Great Britain had become stronger and France weaker, but they had not settled the question of which nation would be greater in North America.

For the longest period in decades, the fighting stopped between the French and British colonies. For thirty-one years, Britain and France were at peace—not because they were friends but because, for the moment, peace had more to offer than war. France needed time to recover its old strength. England, a nation on the rise, needed time to strengthen its growing empire.

In America, the British and French colonies grew. The population of the British colonies rose from less than 500,000 in 1720 to 1.5 million in 1760. The colonists cleared new lands and, in some places, moved west across the Appalachian Mountains. A new colony, Georgia, was founded in 1733 between South Carolina and Spanish Florida. It brought the number of British colonies to thirteen.

More than 90 percent of the colonists made their living from the land. Others lived in cities—such as Boston, New York, and Philadelphia—that were starting their own industries, newspapers, and colleges. Colonial farms produced crops that were in high demand in Europe. Families that owned large tracts of land or built ships to carry exports grew wealthy. Most small farmers and servants, along with thousands of slaves, remained poor.

England wanted to make sure that the colonists, rich or poor, served the interests of their parent country. This was in keeping with mercantilism, an economic system then widely practiced in Europe. Under mercantilism, each country tried to increase its wealth and power by increasing its stores of gold and silver. To accumulate gold and silver, a nation sought to export more goods than it imported. A nation's colonies were supposed to help by producing raw materials for the parent country and buying that country's manufactured goods.

In the British colonies, mercantilism was expressed in a series of laws called the Acts of Trade and Navigation. For example, the colonies were not allowed to sell their own manufactured goods abroad, and some crops could be sold only to England. The trade laws were weakly enforced, and many colonial merchants smuggled goods anywhere they pleased. England, for the most part, left the colonies alone, and the colonies prospered.

New France also grew stronger during the long peace. The population rose from about 15,000 in 1700 to 70,000 in 1763. Those numbers were always 20 to 30 times smaller than the numbers in the English colonies. Still, New France extended its borders. Deep in the wilderness of North America, the French built a chain of forts and trading posts: westward to the Great Lakes and beyond; southward into the Illinois country. Even farther south, in 1718, the French founded New Orleans at the mouth of the Mississippi River, in the province called Louisiana.

The Mississippi was important because it flowed into the warm waters of the Gulf of Mexico. It gave the French a seaport for the winter months when the St. Lawrence River was locked by ice.

French surveyors lay out the city of New Orleans in 1718.

The Mississippi could be used to transport trade goods and supplies. Smaller rivers linked it to many parts of the continent. To control the Mississippi was to control the interior—and block the spread of other countries' colonies.

In 1739, the long peace began to grow shaky. Great Britain went to war with Spain over the right to trade in the Spanish colonies. Britain knew that France would come to the aid of Spain. The British were ready to fight France to see which country would be supreme—not only in America but in places like India and the West Indies, where both nations wanted the rich profits of trade.

In 1740, fighting broke out in another place—central Europe. There, Prussia and Austria went to war over who would inherit the throne of Austria. In

British and colonial troops set off for Louisbourg in April 1745.

this conflict—called the War of the Austrian Succession—France took Prussia's side and Britain took Austria's side. In 1744, France and Britain finally declared war on each other.

For the third time since 1690, war between the European powers led to war in the colonies. In America, it was called King George's War (after George II, then king of England). Once again, the frontier settlements of New England suffered bitter attacks. Once again, the British colonists raised a fleet to sail against Canada. This time they attacked the stone fortress of Louisbourg. During the long peace, the French had built Louisbourg on Cape Breton Island to guard the Gulf of St. Lawrence. Backed by four warships from England, the colonists captured the fortress in April 1745. Three years later, they were forced

to give it back in the treaty that ended the war.

The war decided little of importance in either Europe or America. Tensions were still high between the rival nations; all that was needed was a wind to fan the flames. In 1754, that wind blew from the Ohio Valley.

The valley of the Ohio River was a rich, wooded area where both the French and the British traded for furs. The Ohio River was important to France's empire because it linked Canada and Louisiana. Both France and Britain claimed possession of the valley, but neither had settled it. In 1747, a group of Virginians had formed the Ohio Company to try to change that situation.

The Ohio Company wanted to acquire lands that it could sell to settlers from the English colonies. The British government was happy to have the Ohio Valley settled, in order to cut into France's empire. In 1749, King George II gave the Ohio Company a grant of 500,000 acres. Native Americans of the valley agreed to let the English settle there. The Marquis of Duquesne, governor of New France, decided to keep the English out.

In 1753, Duquesne ordered a line of forts to be built between Lake Erie and the Ohio River. Two of these forts were built—Presqu'Isle and Le Boeuf (both in what is now western Pennsylvania)—before the English told the French to stop. That message was carried by young George Washington, then twenty-one years old and a major in the

Virginia militia. He was sent by Robert Dinwiddie, governor of Virginia and a partner in the Ohio Company. A surveyor and landowner, Washington himself was interested in acquiring new lands. His half-brother Lawrence had been a founding member of the Ohio Company. In October 1753, Washington brought Dinwiddie's letter to the French commander at Fort Le Boeuf. The letter ordered the French to leave. The commander politely said no.

The following year, the French built Fort Duquesne at the forks of the Ohio. This was the most important point in the valley—the place where two smaller rivers join to form the Ohio River. Governor Dinwiddie tried to raise an army to drive the French away, but all he could muster was 150 men, led by George Washington. Washington, now promoted to colonel, had no experience in war.

In May 1754, with Native American allies, Washington's small army reached the Ohio Valley. They soon came upon a band of French troops. The French commander, Coulon de Jumonville, said he had been sent in peace to tell the English to leave. Fighting broke out, and de Jumonville was killed. The French claimed he was murdered, and called for revenge. Over the next few weeks, more than a thousand Canadians and Native Americans massed at Fort Duquesne. Many of the Native Americans had come from what the French called the "Far West" (what we now call the American Midwest). The Potawatomi and the Ottawa, for ex-

WASHINGTON/CUSTIS/LEE COLLECTION, WASHINGTON AND LEE UNIVERSITY, LEXINGTON, VA.

George Washington as painted by Charles Willson Peale.

ample, lived in what is now Michigan and Wisconsin. These tribes would play an important part as French allies in the coming war.

Washington's army was reinforced by more troops from Virginia, but still numbered only 400. They retreated to a clearing called Great Meadows and built a wooden stockade called Fort Necessity. Washington's Native American allies left him, telling him that he had chosen a bad place to make a stand. They were right.

On July 3, the French surrounded Fort Necessity. After a day's battle, Washington was forced to surrender. The next morning—July 4, 1754—the French allowed the English to march the long way back to Virginia. Washington had seen his first battle and his first defeat. He had also fought the first battle of a war that would soon reach around the world.

3

BATTLE FOR EMPIRE

The news of Washington's defeat at Great Meadows shook the governments of Britain and France. Neither country was prepared to go to war, but both were determined to defend their claims in the Ohio Valley. In February 1755, after months of preparation, two regiments of British regulars landed in Virginia—the largest infantry force ever sent from Britain to America.

The 800 troops were under the command of General Edward Braddock, an old, hot-tempered soldier with a reputation for stern discipline. Braddock planned to march his army from Virginia to the Ohio Valley and attack Fort Duquesne. A veteran of European battles, Braddock believed his plan was sound. But Braddock was no longer in Europe.

In America, war was different. One difference was geography. There were

View of the Lines at Lake George, 1759 *by Thomas Davies.*

no roads from Virginia to Fort Duquesne—only the rocky wilderness of the Allegheny Mountains. To cross those mountains, men would have to go ahead of the army cutting trees and blasting rock. Another difference was in the style of fighting. In Europe, soldiers lined up and faced each other across open battlefields. In America, both Canadians and Native Americans were skilled at hiding behind trees and attacking by surprise.

Braddock spent months gathering wagons, horses, and provisions—sometimes without much help from the colonies. His two regiments were each brought up to a full strength of about 700 men; 500 colonial troops joined them. George Washington agreed to serve as Braddock's aide. Unfortunately for Braddock, few Native Americans were recruited. Their knowledge and skill might have helped him in the disaster that followed.

On June 10, 1755, the army set out from Fort Cumberland, Virginia. The

Braddock ambushed by the French and Indians.

column moved slowly on its 110-mile journey, held back by a long wagon train of supplies. A road was cut through the woods; cannons were dragged up mountain slopes. On June 19, Braddock split his army in two: an advance column of 1,400 men traveled ahead, while the remaining 500 men followed at their own pace. On July 9, Braddock's advance column marched within ten miles of Fort Duquesne. They thought that the worst was over and that the actual battle would be easy. But the worst had not yet begun.

The French commander at Fort Duquesne, Pierre de Contrecoeur, sent out a small force to ambush the British soldiers. That force was made up of about 200 French and Canadians and 600 Native Americans. Most of the Native Americans were from "western" tribes such as the Potowatomi and Ottawa, but some were from the Delaware and Shawnee tribes—inhabitants of the Ohio Valley.

Shortly after noon, the British spotted an enemy soldier darting among the trees. Shooting broke out, and the French and Native Americans took cover. Soon they surrounded the British column on three sides, in a U-shape. They fired into the ranks of the British. The greatest slaughter of British soldiers in the history of North America had begun.

The British fired back but could not

see their enemies, who were hidden behind trees and clouds of musket smoke. The red coats of the British, however, were easy targets, as were the officers on their horses. Whooping horribly, the Native Americans took possession of a hilltop and fired from there. The British artillery and supply wagons came up from behind, cutting off retreat. The British were now a terrified mob, packed together while musket balls rained. Washington urged Braddock to let the men take cover, but Braddock refused. Instead he forced the troops to stand in the open, firing uselessly.

Of the 1,400 men in Braddock's command, nearly 1,000 were killed or wounded. Three-fourths of the British officers were killed or wounded. Braddock himself died later of a bullet through his lungs. Women died, too, in the battle: soldiers' wives, known as "necessary women," who had traveled with the army washing clothes and nursing the sick. Of the French and Native Americans, no more than sixty were hurt or killed.

The British survivors fled, leaving everything behind—cannon, ammunition, even Braddock's battle plans. The remaining wagons and supplies were burned to keep them from falling into French hands. What was left of the army retreated to Philadelphia and into winter quarters, though it was only the middle of summer.

For the French, the Battle of the Wilderness (also called Braddock's Defeat) was a spectacular success. For the British, it was a bitter loss. The only conso-

The Burial of Braddock *by Howard Pyle.*

lation for the English colonists that year was a victory on September 8 near Lake George in what is now New York State.

Farther north, in and around the Gulf of St. Lawrence, hostilities had started even before Braddock's Defeat. In June 1755, a British fleet seized two French ships carrying troops to Canada. However, the ships were only a small part of a large fleet that was able to land 3,000 troops safely at Quebec. In the same month, the British captured two forts that threatened the British colony of Nova Scotia in what was once French Acadia.

The British believed Nova Scotia was also in danger from another source—about 10,000 French-speaking Acadians

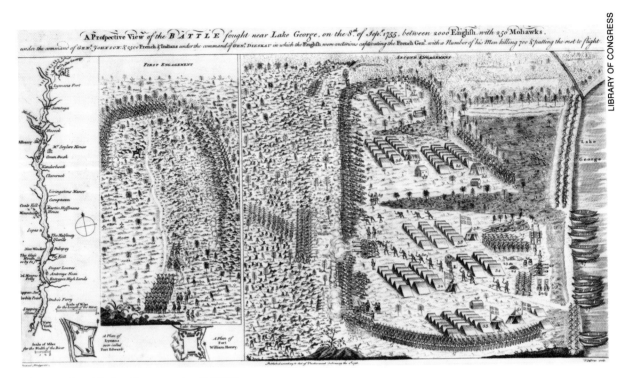

A Prospective View of the BATTLE fought near Lake George, on the 8th of Sept. 1755, between 2000 English, with 250 Mohawks, under the command of Gen. Johnson, & 2500 French & Indians under the command of Gen. Dieskau in which the English were victorious captivating the French Gen. with a Number of his Men killing 700 & putting the rest to flight

The Battle of Lake George, April 1755.

whose families had been there before the British came. Most of these Acadians felt strong ties to France; they had refused over the years to swear an oath of loyalty to Great Britain. Most, however, had stayed neutral during conflicts between the French and British. Even so, the British no longer believed it was safe to let them stay.

In the summer of 1755, about 7,000 Acadians were rounded up and exiled. Their farms were burnt and their possessions taken away. Most Acadians were scattered among the English colonies. Others made their way to Louisiana, where their descendants, the Cajuns (or Acadians), live to the present day.

There were other innocent victims of the undeclared war. With the British army in winter quarters, the long frontier of the British colonies was undefended. War parties made up of Canadians and American Indians—most of them Delaware and Shawnee—came out of the Ohio Valley and crossed the Allegheny Mountains. They attacked settlements in Pennsylvania, Maryland, and Virginia, killing or capturing hundreds of people.

Some colonists fought back by learning Native American and Canadian techniques of forest fighting. Known as rangers, skilled in ambush and swift raids, these men were a distinctly American breed of fighters. They were often as cruel as their enemy, killing and scalping unarmed people, and burning whole villages. Their most famous leader was Robert Rogers, who formed a company called Rogers' Rangers in 1755. Companies such as his soon became an important part of British forces in America.

Despite such efforts at self-defense, the colonies remained weakened by their inability to unite in a common cause. At a conference in Albany in the summer of 1754, a respected Pennsylvanian named Benjamin Franklin had tried to solve that problem. Representatives from six British colonies attended the Albany Congress, which had been called to patch up the English alliance with the Iroquois League. Franklin took the opportunity to suggest a plan for joining together against the French

threat. The representatives at the conference approved the plan, but the colonial assemblies did not. The colonies feared that a strong central government would endanger their freedom. The British crown was relieved; it feared that the colonies, if united, would become more independent. The crown was right. When the colonies finally united two decades later, they were able to become a free nation.

For the time being, the colonies remained separate. In the meantime, England and France, still technically at peace, headed toward a formal declaration of war. In May 1756, after a naval battle at Minorca in the Mediterranean

Benjamin Franklin designed this cartoon to show his support of the Albany Convention's call for colonial unity.

A contemporary portrait of the Marquis de Montcalm.

Sea, that declaration came. Fighting grew more heated in North America, while also spreading to the West Indies and as far east as India. The war that began in the Ohio Valley had become a worldwide battle for empire.

The war between France and England soon became linked to a separate conflict in central Europe. There, relations between Prussia and Austria had stayed tense since the last war. In August 1756, a new struggle broke out when Frederick the Great of Prussia invaded Saxony, a small German state allied to Austria. France, Russia, Sweden, and a few German states took Austria's side, while England helped Prussia with money. The French-English conflict was now one part of what became known as the Seven Years' War. Some historians consider it the first world war.

In America, it was a war that the British were losing. In August 1756, French forces captured Oswego, an important British outpost on Lake Ontario in the colony of New York. The following year, a British expedition against the island fortress of Louisbourg in the gulf of the St. Lawrence River was begun, delayed, and finally called off. In the meantime, the French attacked the site of the only major British victory so far—Lake George. In the summer of 1757, the French not only captured Fort William Henry, near Lake George, but allowed their Native American allies—the Potawatomi, Ottawa, Chippewa, Abnaki, and others—to carry out a massacre. These Native Americans killed, scalped, and took captive hundreds of British prisoners who had been guaranteed fair treatment. The massacre enraged British colonists, not only against the French and Native Americans but against their own commanders as well, who seemed unable to defend the colonies.

The French were led by a brilliant campaigner: Louis Joseph, the Marquis de Montcalm. Montcalm, a small, restless veteran of forty-four, had commanded French regular troops in Canada since 1756. Montcalm was a skillful general, though several factors weakened his command. He often disagreed with Canada's governor, the Marquis Pierre de Vaudreuil, about how to run the war, and was not given full military authority until 1758. He also disliked Canada and doubted that the colony could be defended. Still, his early successes made Canadians confident of victory.

The British, in contrast, were led in 1756–57 by a weak commander in chief named John Campbell, the Earl of Loudoun. Slow and methodical, Loudoun made plans and organized a supply system while Montcalm won battles. Worse still, Loudoun brought new demands from England that angered the colonists. Since these demands were meant to help Britain win the war, Loudoun expected the colonists to comply willingly. But the colonists saw the demands as attacks on their freedom.

Perhaps the most direct attack was impressment, the seizure of civilians to serve in the armed forces. "Impressment gangs" walked the waterfronts of cities like Boston and New York, grabbing workers and forcing them onto warships. Loudoun also demanded supplies and quartering, or shelter, for his men. When the colonies were slow in delivering these, Loudoun threatened to take them by force. He also imposed trade restrictions that were meant to keep provisions from falling into French hands. For a time, an embargo, a prohibition against shipping, closed down all ports from Virginia to New England.

The colonists fought back against Loudoun's measures with every means they had—speeches, newspaper articles, protest in the streets, sometimes even gun battles. Some colonists began to feel that the British were more dangerous to their liberty than the French. The colonists might not have minded as

William Pitt, Britain's leader during the French and Indian War.

much if Loudoun had been winning the war, but Loudoun was losing. When he was finally ordered back to England in December 1757, the colonists rejoiced. Their joy grew greater as the tide of battle began to turn.

The key to the change in fortunes was a new British minister, William Pitt, who came firmly to power in 1757. Pitt was determined to drive the French out of North America by any means necessary. He enlisted more troops and, for the first time, sent most of them to America. He raised taxes in Britain and took out loans to pay for the war. He put young, talented officers in charge and fired generals who proved unworthy. He gained the full support of the colonies by supplying arms, equipment, and money for the regiments they raised.

General Abercrombie's troops charge Fort Ticonderoga in 1758.

Pitt's greatest contribution, however, may have been the new strategy he laid out. It was his plan to strike at the very heart of New France—Quebec. First, however, Quebec's lifelines to the rest of New France would have to be cut. That meant getting control of the three approaches to Quebec, all guarded by French forts—Lake Champlain, the Great Lakes, and the Gulf of St. Lawrence. The first objective, in July 1758, was Fort Ticonderoga on Lake Champlain.

For the British, the battle was a disaster. General James Abercrombie made mistakes in timing and strategy that allowed the French army to beat a force nearly five times larger. Abercrombie was soon recalled, and the British fared better on the Great Lakes route. There, in August, an army composed mostly of colonial soldiers captured Fort Frontenac in what is now the province of Ontario, Canada. Artillery and food supplies were seized, and Lake Ontario was cleared of French ships. Quebec's links to its forts, trading posts, and allies in the west were cut off with one blow.

The Gulf of St. Lawrence was the most important approach to Quebec, and it was guarded by Louisbourg. In July 1758, an expedition from England led by a new commander in chief, General Jeffrey Amherst, captured that fortress. Later that year, a British army marched to the place where the war had started—the forks of the Ohio River. When the British reached Fort Duquesne in November, they found only ruins: the French had blown it up. The British built a new fort and named it after William Pitt. Today the city of Pittsburgh stands on that spot.

Not all victories that year were won by arms. France's Native American allies in the Ohio Valley—the Delaware and Shawnee nations—were stopped from aiding the Canadians by peaceful negotiation. The leaders in these talks were Pennsylvania's Quakers, members of a religious sect whose teachings forbid the use of armed force. The Quakers addressed the complaints Native Americans had about land fraud and other abuses. In the Treaty of Easton in October 1758, the Ohio Valley tribes and the British made peace, and the fall of Fort Duquesne became possible.

The following year, Great Britain's armies closed in on Quebec. On July 25, 1759, a force of British regulars and Iroquois warriors took Fort Niagara, an important French outpost on the Great Lakes. General Amherst's army seized control of Lake Champlain by taking Ticonderoga on July 26 and Crown Point on July 31. The British now stood at two of the three gateways to Quebec. But the decisive campaign would take place along the third.

In June 1759, a fleet of over 200 ships entered the mouth of the St. Lawrence River. Carrying nearly 9,000 troops, it was the largest British fleet ever to cross the Atlantic. The passage up the St. Lawrence was treacherous, full of rocks and shallows, but the ships made it through. In late June, they dropped anchor off the Isle d'Orléans, just downriver from Quebec. The British secured the island as a base. From there General James Wolfe, the young commander of the expedition, looked up at the city. Quebec had not fallen in battle for 130 years. It was up to Wolfe to take it now.

General Amherst, with General Wolfe, directs attack on Louisbourg.

Although slight this is the most convincing portrait of Wolfe
I have ever seen. Cf. Schaaks profile. K Wright. 1864.

to Isaac Barré
from his friend
Geo: Townshend

4

THE END OF AN EMPIRE

At about midnight on June 28, 1759, the British soldiers camped on the Isle d'Orléans got a taste of what the French had in store for them. Under cover of darkness, seven ships floated toward the British fleet anchored in the St. Lawrence River. All at once, the seven vessels exploded in flame. They were unmanned fire ships. Loaded with flammable material, they had been sent out from Quebec to set fire to the British fleet.

The plan didn't work: the fuses had been lit too early. Some of the vessels drifted ashore or were towed away, doing nothing worse than providing a grand fireworks show.

The first line of French defense had failed, but other, more important defenses stood firm. The strongest was Quebec's geography. The cliffs on which Quebec was built stretched for miles east and west along the north bank of the St. Lawrence. The bluffs were 350 feet tall at their highest point. It was true that a part of Quebec—the houses and warehouses of the Lower Town—lay unprotected on the shore. But the Upper Town—the site of the governor's palace—was safe on the heights.

River barriers also protected Quebec: the St. Lawrence River to the south, the Cap Rouge River eight miles west, the St. Charles River directly east, the Montmorency River farther east. Quebec's weakest side was right outside its southwest wall, where a flat, grassy area called the Plains of Abraham offered an easy approach. But to reach the plains, an army would first have to climb the cliffs.

Quebec's natural defenses were strengthened by artificial ones. Montcalm, the French commander in chief, had about 15,000 troops—regulars, militia, and Native Americans—in and around the city. Most were stationed east of Quebec as far as the Montmo-

Major General James Wolfe *by George Townshend.*

Quebec in the mid-seventeenth century.

rency River's narrow, 80-foot falls, with the army's central camp at a village called Beauport. West of the city, a string of garrisons kept watch all the way to the Cap Rouge River.

Quebec was well defended, but Montcalm still doubted that the colony could be saved. Indeed, he was so convinced that Quebec would fall that he kept his main supply base 50 miles to the west, so that the British could not capture it if they took Quebec. But that precaution endangered Quebec, because the British could starve the city simply by cutting the supply line.

Unlike Montcalm, Wolfe intended to win. Although only 32, he had earned a great reputation as a commander at battles such as Louisbourg. Now he was in charge of the most important expedition of the war. Wolfe was tall and red-haired, well versed in the art of war. He was also constantly sick with kidney disease and rheumatism, among other illnesses. The danger of dying from sickness made him unconcerned about dying in battle. Death in victory would be the best of all.

If victory were going to come at Quebec, it would have to come fast. Winter arrived early on the St. Lawrence; the British fleet had to leave by October or be trapped in the frozen river until spring. That meant bold actions were needed. A way had to be found to break through the city's defenses. A way had to be found to provoke Montcalm into battle.

Wolfe's first action was to seize Point Levi on the south bank of the St. Lawrence, facing Quebec. Montcalm had left that bank weakly defended; Wolfe's

Much of Quebec, including the church of Nôtre Dame de la Victoire, lay in ruins after the British bombardment.

men overran it in a short battle on June 30. By early July, batteries of cannon had been aimed at the city from Point Levi. The main body of Wolfe's army moved to the north bank of the St. Lawrence. There they set up camp on the east side of the Montmorency River and stared at the French troops on the other side.

Wolfe had laid siege to the city, but he had not found a way in. In the meantime, he decided to do as much damage as he could. On the night of July 12, the artillery at Point Levi fired on Quebec. Cannonballs and explosives rained on the city, starting fires, destroying homes. The bombardment went on for weeks; by August, 29 artillery pieces had torn apart both the Upper and Lower towns. Half the city's houses, along with its cathedral, burned to the ground.

The bombardment served little military purpose, but it terrified Quebec's citizens and reduced their will to resist. It did not affect Montcalm's army or succeed in forcing Montcalm to fight.

In the countryside, Wolfe ordered a different kind of terror. Since their arrival, the British had been harried by raiders lurking in the woods. Wolfe responded by ordering scouting parties to "burn and lay waste the country." By September, more than 1,400 houses and much farmland had been burned. Wolfe's tactics resulted in fear and suffering but not victory. Victory could come only through an open battle with Montcalm's troops.

On July 31, Wolfe tried to start such a battle at the mud flats just west of the Montmorency River. A wave of soldiers, transported by flatboats, was supposed

45

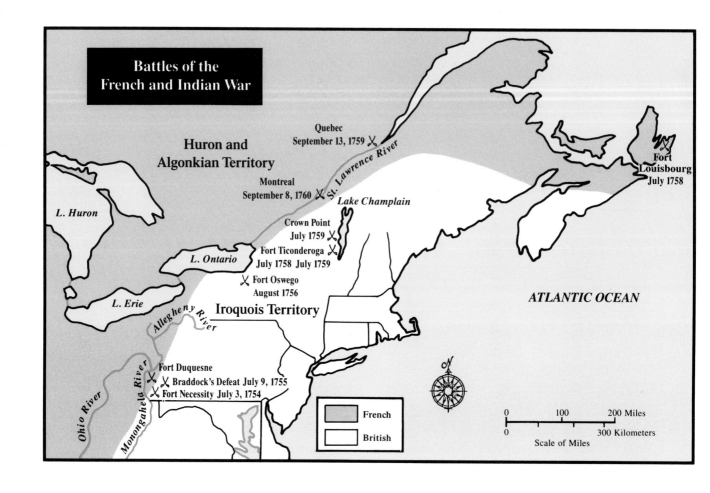

Battles of the
French and Indian War

Huron and
Algonkian Territory

Quebec
September 13, 1759

St. Lawrence River

Montreal
September 8, 1760

Lake Champlain

L. Huron

Crown Point
July 1759

Fort Ticonderoga
July 1758 July 1759

L. Ontario

Fort Oswego
August 1756

L. Erie

Iroquois Territory

Alleghe ny River

ATLANTIC OCEAN

Fort
Louisbourg
July 1758

Ohio River

Monongahela River

Fort Duquesne
Braddock's Defeat July 9, 1755
Fort Necessity July 3, 1754

French

British

N

0   100   200 Miles
0   300 Kilometers
Scale of Miles

to capture several batteries and force the French to respond. The attempt was a disaster: disorder among the troops and a sudden thunderstorm made the British easy targets. Nearly 500 men were killed or wounded, and Wolfe's army retreated.

The hot summer weeks wore on. Many British soldiers deserted to the enemy; hundreds grew sick with dysentery and scurvy. Wolfe himself became ill with a high fever that threatened his life. Desertions were high in the French camp, too, and rations were low. But time was on Montcalm's side: all he had to do was keep his men in the trenches until winter forced the British to leave.

September came. Wolfe recovered partially from his illnesses, but he wrote to Pitt that he was still "at a loss" on how to proceed. Finally, his senior officers, including Admiral Charles Saunders, suggested a plan: the British should land at a point west of Quebec, where the cliffs were most thinly guarded. There they would cut the French supply line and force Montcalm into battle. Wolfe accepted the plan, and preparations were made.

The main body of the army was moved from Montmorency to Point Levi. Saunders moved most of the ships and many of the troops upriver near Cap Rouge. Seeing that an attack might be coming, Montcalm strengthened his detachment at Cap Rouge to 3,000 men under Captain Louis Antoine de Bougainville.

A few days before the attack, Wolfe chose a landing place: a small cove, or recess in the shoreline, two miles west of Quebec. A narrow path led from this inlet (called the Anse au Foulon, and later renamed Wolfe's Cove) to the top of the cliffs. Thinking the path unimportant, Montcalm had posted only a light guard at the top. Wolfe meant to make him regret it.

Just before dawn on September 13, 1759, thirty flatboats containing some 1,600 men floated silently downriver toward the Anse au Foulon. They were the first wave of an army of 4,500. The light infantry on the lead boat soon scrambled up the cliff and overpowered the guards. At the same instant, ships several miles away fired their cannon at Beauport, where Montcalm was camped. The cannonade fooled Montcalm into thinking that the British were attacking east of the city rather than west. By the time word came of the actual landing, it was too late. Montcalm rode into Quebec just before seven in the morning, only to see the bright red coats of Wolfe's soldiers lined up in the morning rain on the Plains of Abraham.

Some 3,300 British stood in a double row facing the city walls. Reserves of 1,200 waited not far away. French snipers fired from the bushes, killing some. Wolfe himself was shot in the wrist, but he kept his position along with his men. Wolfe's meaning was clear: he was daring Montcalm to come out and fight.

It was an awful gamble. The British threatened Montcalm's supply line but had not completely cut it; Montcalm could still put off the battle. Reinforcements for the French were on the way: Bougainville's men were already marching from Cap Rouge toward the rear of Wolfe's army. But for reasons still unknown, Montcalm chose not to wait for Bougainville. Perhaps he had made up his mind that Quebec was doomed. Perhaps he simply made a mistake.

Montcalm ordered an army of 3,000 regulars and 1,500 militia to form in ranks facing the British. Most of them lacked the training and discipline of the British troops. At about ten o'clock, the French advanced. They marched in three columns of white uniforms toward the British line. They started firing

A contemporary engraving of the British attack on Quebec.

when they were more than 100 yards away. At that distance, few British soldiers were hit. The others kept their places, waiting for orders. When the French were 40 yards away, the order came. Thousands of British muskets fired. At that distance, the shots were deadly.

Smoke rose over the battlefield, along with screams of pain. The British reloaded and fired again. The smoke cleared; the French were backing away. Wolfe gave the order to charge. The muskets were not reloaded; the men ran forward, chasing the enemy with the 18-inch blades of their bayonets. The Scots Highlanders used a different weapon—the claymore, a two-edged broadsword. In fifteen minutes the battle was over; Montcalm's army was routed. The British suffered about 660 casualties, the French at least that many, perhaps up to 1,500.

Among the casualties were the two commanding officers: Wolfe and Montcalm. Wolfe had recklessly fought in the front line, where no major-general was supposed to be. Perhaps he had decided that this was the battle where he wanted to die. If so, he got his wish. He was shot through the chest and died moments later on the field of victory.

The defeated general took longer to die. Shot in the stomach, Montcalm rode back into Quebec with his retreating army. After a night of pain, he died early next morning.

The remainder of the army, with Governor Vaudreuil, escaped to Montreal by a road that the British had left

The Death of General Wolfe *by Benjamin West*.

open. On September 18, the citizens of Quebec surrendered. The capital of New France had fallen. The fate of North America, it seemed, had been decided in 15 minutes of battle. But that fate was not yet sealed. Montreal still stood, and the French army was still free. The British who had taken Quebec now had to prove they could keep it.

Seven thousand British troops stayed in Quebec through the winter. When spring came, so did the French. In April 1760, General François Gaston de Lévis marched with about 7,000 men from Montreal. A second battle was fought on the Plains of Abraham, and this time the British lost. General Murray's men were forced back into the city while de Lévis laid siege. Then, in May, a ship came into view—a British ship, carrying

supplies and reinforcements. More ships followed, and de Lévis retreated. Quebec stayed in British hands.

In the summer of 1760, three British armies approached Canada's last stronghold—Montreal. Murray's men came up the St. Lawrence from Quebec; another army from Lake Champlain; another from the Great Lakes. By September, Montreal was surrounded by the enemy. The city's troops had deserted in large numbers; only about 2,000 men were left to face an army of 17,000. On September 8, Governor Vaudreuil signed the papers of surrender. Canada belonged to the British.

The war in America was all but over. There was still some fighting—an uprising of the Cherokee nation in 1760–61 in what is now Tennessee; and a battle

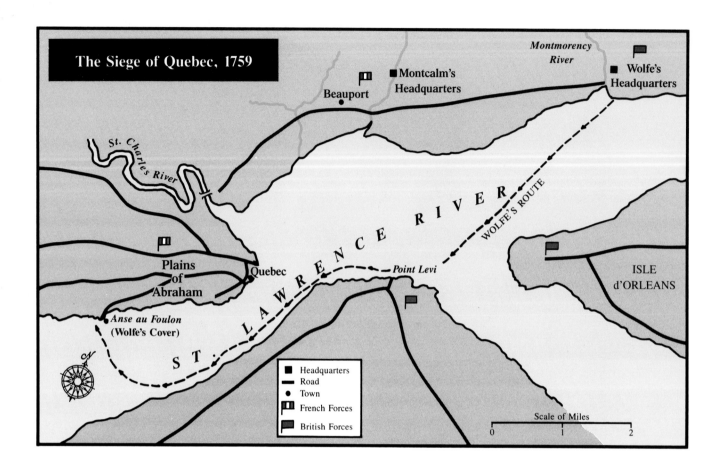

The Siege of Quebec, 1759

Montmorency River

Wolfe's Headquarters

Beauport

Montcalm's Headquarters

St. Charles River

WOLFE'S ROUTE

Plains of Abraham

Quebec

Point Levi

ISLE d'ORLEANS

Anse au Foulon (Wolfe's Cove)

ST. LAWRENCE RIVER

Headquarters
Road
Town
French Forces
British Forces

Scale of Miles
0   1   2

in Newfoundland in 1762. But for the most part, Commander in Chief Amherst waited for the war overseas to end.

That war had also turned in favor of the British. The year 1759 was known as England's "wonderful year." Besides Quebec, the British won victories that year at Guadeloupe in the West Indies and Madras in India; and naval battles near Lagos in West Africa and at Quiberon Bay off France. Britain faced a new danger in 1762, when Spain entered the war on the French side. That threat was met when the British seized the Spanish colonial cities of Havana in Cuba and Manila in the Philippines.

Meanwhile, on the continent of Europe, Britain's ally Prussia fought its many enemies to a stalemate. In 1762, Prussia made a separate peace with Russia and Sweden. All of the nations still at war—including England and France—came to terms in the Peace of Paris in 1763.

The Peace of Paris established Great Britain as the world's greatest colonial power. France was forced to give up most of its American empire—keeping only some possessions in the West Indies, fishing rights in the Gulf of St. Lawrence, and two small islands off Newfoundland. The British gained the rest of Canada, along with all North America east of the Mississippi River.

Britannia	Mars	Neptune	Genius of France	Mons.ʳ Le Politicien	Jack Tar
Your Conquering Arms declare high Heaven is pleas'd, And sanctifies The Justice of your Cause. Maintain your Rights: Be Britons, and be Brave.	This for the Honour of The British Sword. Drawn by my Lawfull and much injured Son.	This for the Honour of The British Flag Conducted by the Nobly-Spirited Anson.	Ave Maria, que jerens Nous: after our Massacres and Persecutions. Must Hereticks possess this promis'd Land, which we so piously have call'd our Own!	garni bleu! had not been lost in a Fog. We should have Trompe Les foules Angloises out of tout L' Amerique Septentrional.	Hark ye Mounseer! was that your Map of North America! what a vast tract of Land you had! pity the Right Owner should take it from you.

BRITAIN's RIGHTS maintaind; or FRENCH AMBITION dismantled.

This cartoon celebrates Britain's victory over France in North America and around the world.

Louisiana west of the Mississippi River was given to Spain. Spain recovered Havana and Manila, but was forced to give Florida to Britain. On the other side of the world, the British took over French claims in India.

Great Britain's North American empire now stretched from the Arctic Circle to the Gulf of Mexico, from the Atlantic Ocean to the Mississippi River. But England's troubles were not over. The gaining of new lands would soon contribute to the loss of older and more valued possessions—the thirteen colonies on the Atlantic seaboard.

The thirteen colonies had always depended on England to defend them against New France. Without that hostile neighbor, independence became a possibility. In addition, the French and Indian War gave the colonies a new confidence in their own military skill. It was Great Britain's regular troops and royal navy that had crushed New France. But the colonists tended to give the credit to their own soldiers and rangers.

The colonies might have remained united with Great Britain if life had gone back to the way it was before the war. In those days, Britain had observed a policy called "salutary neglect"—leaving the colonies alone and letting them prosper. But war had changed things. Loudoun and other commanders had

THE HORSE AMERICA, *throwing his Master.*

Pub.ᵈ as the Act directs, Aug.ᵗ 1.ᵗ 1779, by M.ʳˢ White, Angel Court, Westminster.

This cartoon depicts Britain's rebellious American colonies as a horse throwing its "master."

carried out measures that interfered with colonial life—sharper restrictions on trade; quartering; impressment. It soon became clear that the British meant to keep interfering.

One source of conflict was taxation. The war had left Britain with a national debt of 140 million pounds. Britain expected the colonies to help pay off the debt. Parliament passed a series of laws levying taxes and imposing duties on imports. The Revenue Act of 1764 taxed foreign goods such as sugar, wine, and silk. The Stamp Act of 1765 required many kinds of documents to be stamped at a price.

The colonists were not used to such taxes. Some argued that Parliament had no right to tax the colonies, since the colonies were not represented in the British government. Parliament repealed the Stamp Act, but it also stated firmly, in the Declaratory Act of 1766, that it had "full power and authority" over the colonies. King George III asserted his authority, too. Colonial governors were told to enforce royal prerogative—the right of a king to command—at the expense of elected assemblies. Judges were told they held their jobs at the king's "will and pleasure."

The authority of both Parliament and king was backed up by a standing army of 10,000 troops. This army had been left in America after the war for the stated purpose of defending the new territories. But it also served to guard against the resistance of colonists.

There was some need for defense of the new territories. From 1763 to 1764, an Ottawa warrior named Pontiac led an uprising of Native American tribes from the Ohio Valley to the Illinois country. The tribes were angered by the British refusal to treat them with the respect and generosity the French had shown. Pontiac's Rebellion was crushed, but the British feared it might happen again. The Royal Proclamation of 1763 tried to reduce tensions with Native Americans. Trade with Native Americans was put under royal control. Colonists were forbidden to move west of the Appalachians, where they might disturb Native American land. The decree was weakly enforced, but settlers and speculators (people who bought and sold land for profit) denounced it as another example of British oppression.

The conflict between the colonies and Great Britain grew more heated as the years went on. Colonial resistance took many forms—boycotts, demonstrations, violence, publications, destruction of taxed property (as in the "tea parties" protesting the tax on tea). The British government cracked down. Harsher laws were passed, ending in the so-called Intolerable Acts of 1774. In 1775, resistance finally took the form of war when colonial militia fought British troops at Lexington and Concord. The following year, on July 4, the break with England became complete. The Second Continental Congress declared that the colonies were now "free and independent states."

A colonial newspaper protests the Stamp Act.

In the War of Independence that followed, France took its revenge for the fall of Quebec. France supplied the American rebels with equipment, money, troops, and naval support. France's help was decisive at Yorktown in 1781, the last major battle of the war in North America. Spain and the Netherlands, fearing that the last war had made Britain too powerful, also joined the fighting. The war spread to the West Indies, India, and the Mediterranean. For Britain, the price of victory in one war was defeat in the next.

The Americans were not especially concerned with events overseas. In the Treaty of Paris of 1783, they got what they wanted—recognition that the thirteen colonies were now the United States of America.

The long history of European conflicts went on; England and France remained rivals. Far away, the United States had begun a history of its own.

AFTERWORD

THE SHAPING OF A CONTINENT

The consequences of the fall of Quebec did not end when the United States gained its independence. The French and Indian War shaped the history of North America in at least three other ways. First, it put Great Britain in possession of Canada. Second, it meant that Native Americans east of the Mississippi would have to deal with British Canada and the United States instead of with New France. Finally, the war left a population of French-speaking Canadians who have struggled to keep their identity to the present day.

The United States came into being with its recent enemy, Great Britain, still controlling the territory to the north. That fact made for tense relations between the United States and Canada. During the War of Independence, American armies captured Montreal

Quebec City today.

and unsuccessfully laid siege to Quebec. The British used Canada as a base for attacks on New York. After that war, Canada provided a refuge for some 40,000 Americans who had stayed loyal to Britain.

The Treaty of Paris of 1783 officially ended the war between the United States and Great Britain. It defined the border between the United States and Canada (also called British North America), but it left many people dissatisfied. The United States was given the territory from the Appalachians to the Mississippi River, including the Ohio Valley—an amount that seemed far too generous to some Canadians. Americans were annoyed that the British maintained several forts on American land—for example, at Detroit and Niagara. Those forts were given up in 1794–95, but Americans continued to accuse the British of encouraging Native American attacks.

PAR SON EXCELLENCE

GEORGE WASHINGTON,

Commandant en Chef des Armées Des Provinces unies de
L'Amerique Septentrionale.

AUX PEUPLES DE CANADA.

AMIS & FRERES,

LA Conteste denaturé entre les Colonies Ameriquaines, et Grande Bretagne est arrivé à un point, que ses Armes seules peuvent la decider. Les Colonies, se fiant à la Justice de leur Cause, & la pureté de leurs Intentions, sont obligé avec Repugnance, de recourir à cet Etre qui regle tous les Evenemens humains. Jusqu'ici il a Beni leurs vertueux Efforts; La Main de la Tyrannie est arreté dans le Cours de ses Ravages, & les Armes Brittaniques, qui ont Brillée avec tant d'Eclat dans tous les Parties du Monde, se font ternies, disgraciées et frustrées. Des Generaux de la plus haute Experience, et qui se sont vantez de subjuguer ce grand Continent, se trouvent resserrez entre les Murailles d'une seule Ville & de ses Fauxbourgs, souffrants toute la Honte & la Detresse d'un Siege.—Tandis que les Enfans de l'Amerique animés par l'Amour de la Patrie et le principe de la Liberté generale, s'unissent de plus en plus, chaque Jour se perfectionnent en Discipline, repoussent avec Courage toutes les Attaques & meprisent touts les Dangers. Nous, nous rejouissons sur tout que nos Enemis sont trompez a votre Egard. Ils se sont flattés, ils ont osé dire que le Peuple de Canada ne furent nullement capables de distinguer entre les Douceurs de la Liberté, et la Misere de Servitude; qu'on n'avoit qu'a flatter la Vanité d'un petit Nombre de votre Noblesse, pour eblouir les yeux des Canadiens. Ils ont cru par cette Artifice vous rendre faciles a toutes leur Vues. Mais ils se sont heureusement trompez, au Lieu de trouver en vous, cette Bassesse d'Ame, & pauvreté d'Esprit, ils voient avec un Chagrin egal a notre joie que vous etes Hommes eclarés, genereux, et vertueux, que vous ne voulez ni renoncer à vos propres Droits, ni servir en Instruments pour en priver les autres.

Venez donc, nos chers Confreres, unissons nous dans un Noeud indissoluble, courons ensemble au meme But. Nous avons pris les Armes en Defense de nos Biens, de Notre Liberté, de nos Femmes & nos Enfans—Nous sommes determinés de les conserver, ou de mourir. Nous regardons avec Plaisir ce Jour, peu eloigné (comme nous esperons) quand touts les Habitans de L'Amerique auront le meme Sentiment et jouiront des Douceurs d'un libre Gouvernement.

Incité par ces Motifs, et encouragé par l'Avis de plusieurs Amis de la Liberté chez vous, le Grand Congres Ameriquain a fait entrer dans votre Province un Corps de Troupes sous les Ordres du General Schuyler, non a piller, mais a proteger, pour animer et mettre en Action les Sentimens liberaux que vous avez fait voir; et que les Agens du Despotism s'efforcent d'eteindre par tout le Monde. Pour aider ce Dessein, & pour renverser le Projet horrible d'ensanglanter nos Frontieres par le Carnage des Femmes & des Enfans, J'ai fait marcher le Sieur Arnold, Colonel avec un Corps de l'Armée sous mes Ordres pour la Canada. Il est enjoint, et je suis certain qu'il se conformera a ses Instructions de se considerer et d'agir en tout, comme dans le Pais de ses Patrons & meilleurs Amis—Les Necessaires et Munition de toute Sorte que vous lui fournirez, il recevra avec Reconnoissance, et en payera la plein Valeur. Je vous supplie donc comme Amis, et Freres de pourvoir a touts ses Besoins, et Je vous garantis ma Foi et mon Honneur pour un bonne et ample Recompense aussi bien que votre Sureté et Repos. Que Personne abandonne sa Maison a son Approche—Que Personne s'enfuit—La Cause de l'Amerique et de la Liberté est la Cause de tout vertueux Citoyen Ameriquain, quelle soit sa Religion, quelque que soit le Sang dont il tire son Origine. Les Colonies unies ignorent ce que c'est la Distinction hors celle que la Corruption et l'esclavage peuvent produire——Allons donc, chers & generaux Citoyens, rangez vous sous l'Etendard de la Liberté generale que toute la Force et l'Artifice de la Tyrannie ne sera jamais capable d'ebranler.

G. Washington.

BY HIS EXCELLENCY

GEORGE WASHINGTON, Esquire,

Commander in Chief of the Army of the United Colonies of
North-America.

To the INHABITANTS of CANADA.

FRIENDS and BRETHREN,

THE unnatural Contest between the English Colonies and Great-Britain, has now risen to such a Heighth, that Arms alone must decide it. The Colonies, confiding in the Justice of their Cause, and the Purity of their Intentions, have reluctantly appealed to that Being, in whose Hands are all human Events. He has hitherto smiled upon their virtuous Efforts—The Hand of Tyranny has been arrested in its Ravages, and the British Arms which have shone with so much Splendor in every Part of the Globe, are now tarnished with Disgrace and Disappointment.—Generals of approved Experience, who boasted of subduing this great Continent, find themselves circumscribed within the Limits of a single City and its Suburbs, suffering all the Shame and Distress of a Siege. While the freeborn Sons of America, animated by the genuine Principles of Liberty and Love of their Country, with increasing Union, Firmness and Discipline repel every Attack, and despise every Danger.

Above all, we rejoice, that our Enemies have been deceived with Regard to you—They have persuaded themselves, they have even dared to say, that the Canadians were not capable of distinguishing between the Blessings of Liberty, and the Wretchedness of Slavery; that gratifying the Vanity of a little Circle of Nobility—would blind the Eyes of the People of Canada.—By such Artifices they hoped to bend you to their Views, but they have been deceived, instead of finding in you that Poverty of Soul, and Baseness of Spirit, they see with a Chagrin equal to our Joy, that you are enlightned, generous, and virtuous—that you will not renounce your own Rights, or serve as Instruments to deprive your Fellow Subjects of theirs.—Come then, my Brethren, unite with us in an indissoluble Union, let us run together to the same Goal.—We have taken up Arms in Defence of our Liberty, our Property, our Wives, and our Children, we are determined to preserve them, or die. We look forward with Pleasure to that Day not far remote (we hope) when the Inhabitants of America shall have one Sentiment, and the full Enjoyment of the Blessings of a free Government.

Incited by these Motives, and encouraged by the Advice of many Friends of Liberty among you, the Grand American Congress have sent an Army into your Province, under the Command of General Schuyler; not to plunder, but to protect you; to animate, and bring forth into Action those Sentiments of Freedom you have disclosed, and which the Tools of Despotism would extinguish through the whole Creation.—To co-operate with this Design, and to frustrate those cruel and perfidious Schemes, which would deluge our Frontiers with the Blood of Women and Children; I have detached Colonel Arnold into your Country, with a Part of the Army under my Command—I have enjoined upon him, and I am certain that he will consider himself, and act as in the Country of his Patrons, and best Friends. Necessaries and Accommodations of every Kind which you may furnish, he will thankfully receive, and render the full Value.—I invite you therefore as Friends and Brethren, to porvide him with such Supplies as your Country affords; and I pledge myself not only for your Safety and Security, but for ample Compensation. Let no Man desert his Habitation—Let no one flee as before an Enemy. The Cause of America, and of Liberty, is the Cause of every virtuous American Citizen; whatever may be his Religion or his Descent, the United Colonies know no Distinction but such as Slavery, Corruption and arbitrary Domination may create. Come then, ye generous Citizens, range yourselves under the Standard of general Liberty—against which all the Force and Artifice of Tyranny will never be able to prevail.

G. Washington.

George Washington wrote to the people of Canada (in both French and English), hoping that they would join in the thirteen colonies' rebellion against Britain.

Canada's path to independence and unity wasn't smooth. In this 1849 painting, rebels burn the provincial parliament building in Montreal.

Some Americans in the West wanted to expand into Canada. They thought Canadians would be eager to rebel against Britain. The desire to obtain Canada was one of the factors that brought the United States into conflict with Britain in the War of 1812. Other factors included British attacks on American shipping and British impressment of American seamen.

The United States found that Canada was not easily conquered. American invasion attempts during the war were poorly managed; Canadians proved unwilling to surrender. American forces did gain control of the Great Lakes and in 1813 burned down York (now called Toronto)—the capital of the province of Upper Canada (now Ontario). In retaliation, the British burned much of the U.S. capital of Washington the following year.

The treaty that ended the war in 1814 restored the boundaries that existed before the war. It also marked the last time the United States would try to conquer Canada. For Canada, the war acted as a unifying force. Though Canadians were a people of many origins scattered over a long frontier, they had united against a common enemy and begun to form a national identity.

The United States and Britain never fought each other again—though from time to time they came close. One such incident arose in 1846 over ownership of the so-called Oregon Country, the land between Alaska and California west of the Rocky Mountains. The countries agreed to divide the territory, and war was avoided.

Today the boundary between the United States and Canada is the longest undefended border in the world. Disputes about issues such as trade and the environment continue, but they are

Queen Elizabeth signs the new Constitution Act in 1982.

settled peacefully. The two countries are close allies and carry on the world's largest two-way trade.

Canada expanded from coast to coast as the United States did, although its population remains much smaller—25 million, or about one-tenth that of the United States. In terms of land, Canada is 10 percent larger than the United States, but much of that land is almost uninhabitable. Large parts of the east and north are covered by the so-called Canadian Shield of forest and rock. A wintry climate also limits settlement in the north. Most Canadians live within a hundred miles of the U.S. border; 60 percent live in the two provinces of Ontario and Quebec.

Unlike the United States, Canada has kept its formal ties to Great Britain. Those ties, however, grew weaker over the years. In 1867, the British Parliament passed the British North America Act, uniting Canada in a "confederation" and giving it the right to govern its own domestic affairs. In the 1920s, Canada won the right to sign its own treaties and control its own military commitments. In 1982, Britain gave up its last remaining power over Canada—the exclusive right to amend Canada's constitution. Canada, like other dominions, or former colonies, in the Commonwealth, is now a fully independent, self-governing nation. Its government is modeled on the British parliamentary system. Like the other dominions, Canada continues to accept the monarch of Great Britain as its own monarch—Canada's formal head of state.

Both Americans and Canadians have benefited from the history of peaceful relations between their two countries. But at least one group was better off when New France and the thirteen British colonies existed as enemies: Native

Americans. The French had treated Native Americans with respect and seldom took away their lands—unlike British settlers and land speculators. Even so, when the War of Independence came, most Native American tribes fought on the side of the British. They saw the British as their only safeguard against American expansion. They were right.

At first the new United States promised to protect Native American interests. Federal policy stated that Native American land could not be bought or sold except with tribal consent and through treaty with the federal government. United States citizens who squatted, or settled illegally, on Native American land would be punished by the government.

In practice, however, the government did little to stop settlers from moving onto Native American lands. Speculators and state governments put pressure on the federal government to get the Native Americans out. The government did so through a series of treaties. In 1784, the Iroquois signed the first of many such treaties, ceding land in Pennsylvania and New York. In 1795, after a war with U.S. troops, the tribes of the Ohio Valley—the Delaware, Shawnee, and others—ceded much of the present state of Ohio. In theory, each treaty was made with the "consent" of the tribe. But Native Americans had little understanding of the idea of land ownership, and their consent was usually gotten by threats, trickery, or military conquest.

In the 1820s, the federal government came to believe that Native Americans east of the Mississippi should be "removed" west of that river. There the United States could place them in the Louisiana Territory purchased in 1803 from France. The Indian Removal Act of 1830 made that policy official: tribes from Ohio to Florida were forced to sell their lands and go west.

Nearly all the tribes who had fought on both sides of the French and Indian War were forced to go to what are now Oklahoma, Kansas, and Nebraska. The new land was a place of arid plains, very different from the forests that eastern Native Americans were used to. Many died of disease or hunger on the way. The removal of 17,000 Cherokee from Georgia in 1838–39 is known as the Trail of Tears: one in every four died on the way.

The tribes were promised that the new land would be theirs "as long as grass grows or water runs." That promise was not kept. As U.S. settlers pushed west, Native Americans were pushed farther west, onto smaller reservations. Still, a few remnants of the eastern tribes managed to stay in the eastern states. Many Iroquois, for example, still live on reservations in New York State.

The Native American tribes of eastern Canada did not fare much better. By the 1850s they had lost the greater part of their lands—by treaties, by purchases, sometimes simply by being pushed out. In some respects, however,

This painting shows the "Trail of Tears"—the path the Cherokee took when removed from the eastern United States.

Native Americans in Canada were more fortunate than those in the United States. For one thing, they never suffered a "removal" policy. The government of Upper Canada did invite its Native American tribes to move to new territory in 1836. But unlike the United States, Upper Canada did not force them to go when they refused.

Today, Native Americans are recognized as one of Canada's three "founding peoples" (along with the French and English), and they have taken part in revising Canada's constitution in the 1980s. Still, many Native Americans in both Canada and the United States remain poor and continue to suffer discrimination. Tribes in both countries have organized politically to preserve their identity and struggle for their rights.

One other group of Canadians also keeps working to preserve its identity: the French-speaking people whose ancestors were conquered in the French and Indian War. Initially, the British hoped that these 70,000 people would either leave or become used to English colonial culture. In the Royal Proclamation of 1763, British law was introduced and Roman Catholics were forbidden to hold public office. But French Canadians proved unwilling to give up their old ways. Britain—already facing rebellion in its thirteen colonies—soon changed its policy.

The Quebec Act of 1774 granted the free exercise of Roman Catholicism. It upheld French civil law and the Canadian land-holding system. It put the province under the rule of an appointed council. It also angered some people in the thirteen colonies by placing Quebec's southern border at the Ohio River. This border cut off the spread of the English colonies. Quebec's boundaries became smaller after the American Revolution. But Britain continued to recognize the special status of Canada's French-speaking people.

That special status has remained an issue in Canadian politics to the present day. Today, more than 85 percent of people in Quebec speak French as their first language. But in Canada's nine other provinces, English-speaking people are in the majority. People of French ancestry make up only 28 percent of Canada's total population. As a result, the Québecois—the French-speaking people of Quebec—have always had to guard against the loss of their distinct culture.

Since the Dominion of Canada was formed in 1867, Quebec has had equal status with the other provinces. But for most of their history, the Québecois have been poorer and had fewer opportunities than the English-speaking majority. In the past few decades, the Québecois have taken steps to improve their condition and determine their own future.

The first stage of change began around 1960. In what became known as the Quiet Revolution, the Québecois took more control of their province's economy, reformed its educational system, and became more politically active. In the 1960s and 1970s, Quebec separatists argued—sometimes violently—that the province should drop out of the Canadian union altogether. To try to prevent such a division, the national government in 1969 declared Canada a bilingual country—with both French and English as official languages. But in 1976, a separatist party, the Parti Québecois, was elected to lead the province of Quebec.

Louis Joseph Papineau, a French Canadian, led an unsuccessful rebellion against British rule in Quebec in 1837.

For a time it seemed that the Canadian confederation would be torn apart. But in 1980, Quebec held a referendum—a vote by all of the province's citizens—on whether Quebec should become a sovereign state. A majority of the people answered no, and Canada remained united. Conflicts continue between Quebec and the other provinces. But the country is still one.

The survival of the Québecois in Canada is only one of the legacies left by the French and Indian War. The birth of the United States, the rise of modern Canada, the expulsion of Native Americans from eastern North America—all these events were in the wings when Wolfe defeated Montcalm before the walls of Quebec. Perhaps none of these events was destined to happen; perhaps any one of them might have turned out differently. But each of them depended on what came before. Like every great event, the fall of Quebec sent out echoes that are still heard today.

INDEX

Page numbers in *italics* indicate illustrations.

SUGGESTED READING

Hibbert, Christopher. *Wolfe at Quebec*. Cleveland: World Publishing Company, 1959.

Malcolm, Andrew H. *The Canadians*. New York: Times Books, 1985.

Marrin, Albert. *Struggle for a Continent: The French and Indian Wars 1690–1760*. New York: Atheneum, 1987.

Meltzer, Milton. *George Washington and the Birth of Our Nation*. New York: Franklin Watts, 1986.

O'Meara, Walter. *Guns at the Forks*. Englewood Cliffs, N.J.: Prentice-Hall, 1965.

White, Jon M. *Everyday Life of the North American Indian*. New York: Holmes & Meier, 1979.